PHONICS

101 Things Every KINDERGARTNER Should Know About PHONICS

Contributing Writer

Kristen Walsky

Consultant

Dr. Leslie Anne Perry

active minds®

Kristen Walsky received her masters degree in early childhood education from Nova Southeastern University in 2000. She has taught kindergarten for ten years and recently started a new Web site containing materials that serve an academic purpose in kindergarten classrooms. She lives in Florida with her husband, Scott, and her two sons, Davis and Jackson.

Dr. Leslie Anne Perry has been teaching public school for 13 years. Currently, she is a professor in the department of curriculum and instruction at East Tennessee State University, where she teaches language arts and children's literature courses. She also serves as the coordinator for the M.Ed. in elementary education program. She is the author of *Primary Reading and Writing Activities for Every Month of the School Year* and has 65 articles published in 55 different journals and magazines.

Illustrations by **George Ulrich**

Picture credits: **Comstock RF; Corbis RF; Image Club Graphics; PhotoDisc; PIL Collection; StockByte**

ActiveMinds® is a registered trademark of Publications International, Ltd.

Louis Weber, CEO
Publications International, Ltd.
7373 North Cicero Avenue
Lincolnwood, Illinois 60712

www.myactiveminds.com

ISBN-13: 978-1-4127-1618-5
ISBN-10: 1-4127-1618-7

Manufactured in China.

8 7 6 5 4 3 2 1

Contents

Follow the Phonics Path

Dear Parents:

Kindergarten is an exciting time in your child's life. They are excited about learning to read, write, and think independently. Kindergarten children are ready to learn letter sounds and put letters together to form and read words. As a parent, you want to give your child extra experiences that will expose them to phonics skills. This

workbook will teach your child basic phonics skills that they can build on as their reading ability progresses.

Inside this workbook, children will find 101 fun-filled phonics activities. Each activity focuses on a different skill and provides your child with plenty of opportunities to practice that skill. The activities are arranged in order of difficulty, beginning with the most basic skills to build your child's confidence. They will feel a real sense of accomplishment with each completed each page.

Every activity is clearly labeled with the skill being taught. You will find skill keys written especially for you at the bottom of the page. These skills give you information about what your child is learning. Suggestions are also provided for additional hands-on activities and extensions that you may choose to do with your child. These offer fun opportunities to reinforce the skill being taught.

Children learn in a variety of ways. They are sure to be interested in the colorful and engaging illustrations in this workbook. The pictures are vibrant and will assist with comprehension of the words and stories that your child will learn. Children may also like to touch the pictures and say the words out loud. Such methods can be important aids in your child's learning process.

Your child will be able to complete some of the activities independently; however, in some instances, you will need to read the directions to your child before they can complete the activities. Each activity should be fun and rewarding for your child. Be patient and support your child in positive ways—help them rise to the chal-
lenges. Let them know it's all right to take a guess or ask for help if they are unsure. Learning should be an exciting and positive experience for everyone. Celebrate the learning of new sounds and words. Don't forget to enjoy your time together as your child develops his or her kindergarten phonics skills!

My Phonics Book

Your name is special to you. Say the letters in your first name.
Each of the letters in your name makes a different sound.
Sound out your name. Now write your name.

KALEIGH

Answers will vary.

My Alphabet

There are 26 letters in the alphabet. The letters can be written in uppercase and lowercase. **Uppercase** letters are often tall and fat. **Lowercase** letters are often short and thin. Trace each letter and say the name and sound that it makes.

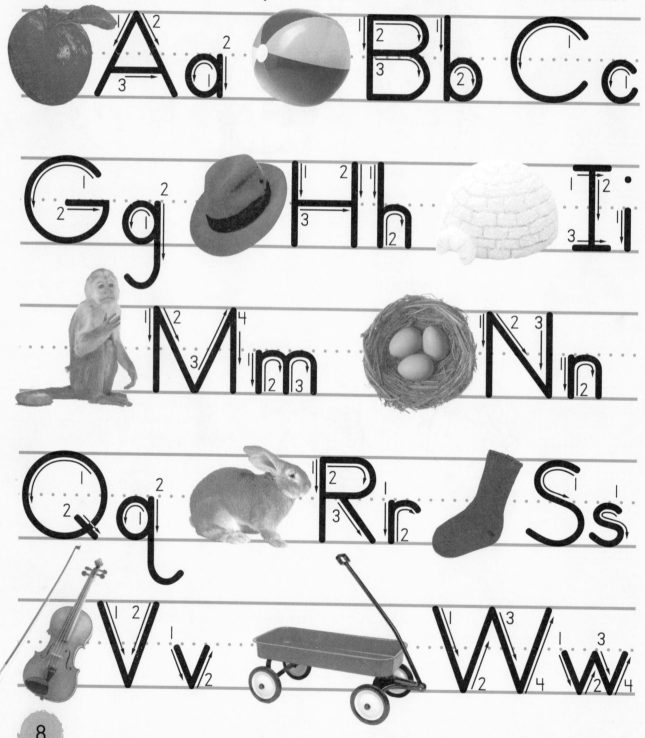

Parents: Say the sounds of the letters and the names of the pictures. Have your child point to the letters that match the sounds.

Skill: Saying and recognizing the sounds that letters make

9

Sounds All Around

Words are made of letters. Learning the 26 letters of the alphabet is part of learning how to read. Let's learn the sounds that each letter makes! Read the poem and underline the words that sound the same. Two have been done for you.

Letters

ABC's and **123**'s

Letters and numbers are different I see.

Letters make words that I can <u>read,</u>

working each day is all I <u>need.</u>

Learning letter sounds is so much fun,

they help me read words like sun and run!

I am reading now, words and books,

a little time is all it took!

Parents: Read the poem to your child. Help them underline the rhyming words.

Skill: Understanding that words are made up of letters and sounds

Answers on page 122.

Uppercase Letters

Capital letters are also called **uppercase** letters. Trace the capital letters in the alphabet blocks below with your finger. Now practice writing the **uppercase** letters on your own. Say the sound of each letter as you write it.

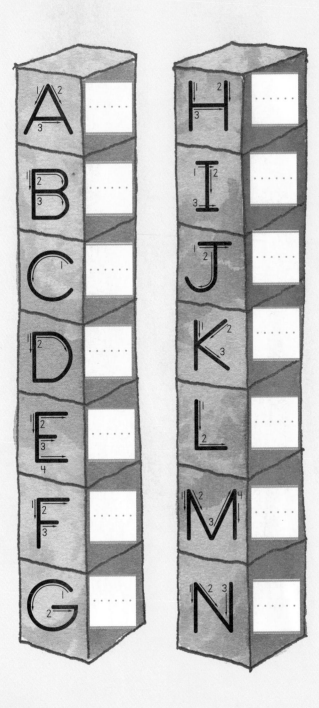

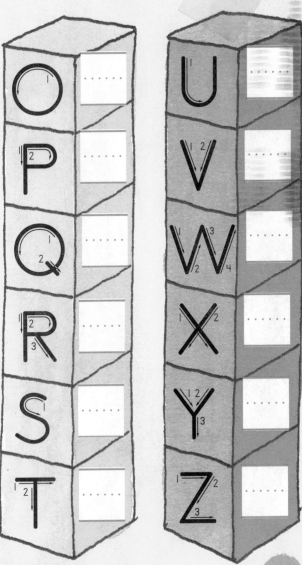

Alphabet Parade

The letters you see in the parade are in alphabetical order. Some of the letters are missing! Follow the parade from left to right and write the missing uppercase letters where they belong.

F G _ H I _ L _ N O _ Q R X Z

Special Names

Uppercase letters are used to show that some words are special. Uppercase letters can be used at the beginning of people's names. In the spaces below, write the names of people in your family. You can even write your name! Be sure to use an uppercase letter at the beginning of each name.

Parents: Guide your child in writing the names of some of the people in your family. Make certain uppercase letters are used only where they should be.

Skill: Capitalizing names

Answers will vary.

Lowercase Letters

Trace the **lowercase** letters in the alphabet blocks below with your finger. Now practice writing the **lowercase** letters on your own. Say the sound of each letter as you write it.

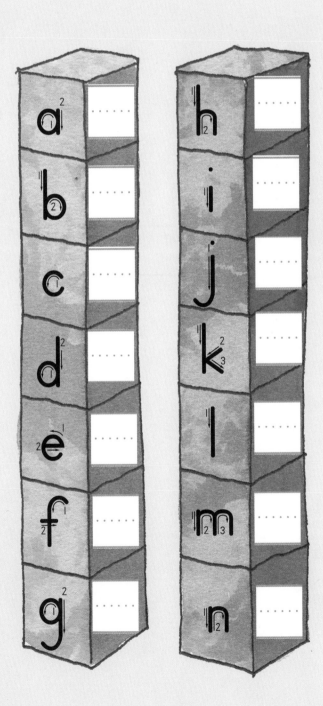

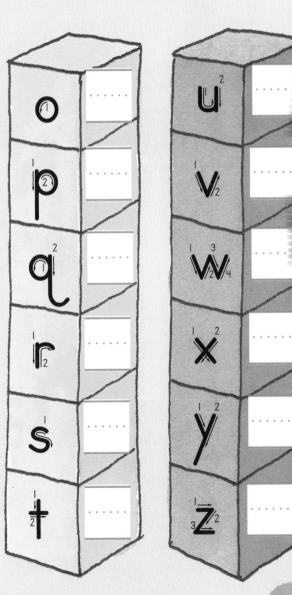

Lowercase Letter Train

The letters on the train are in alphabetical order. Some of the letters are missing! Write the missing lowercase letters on the train.

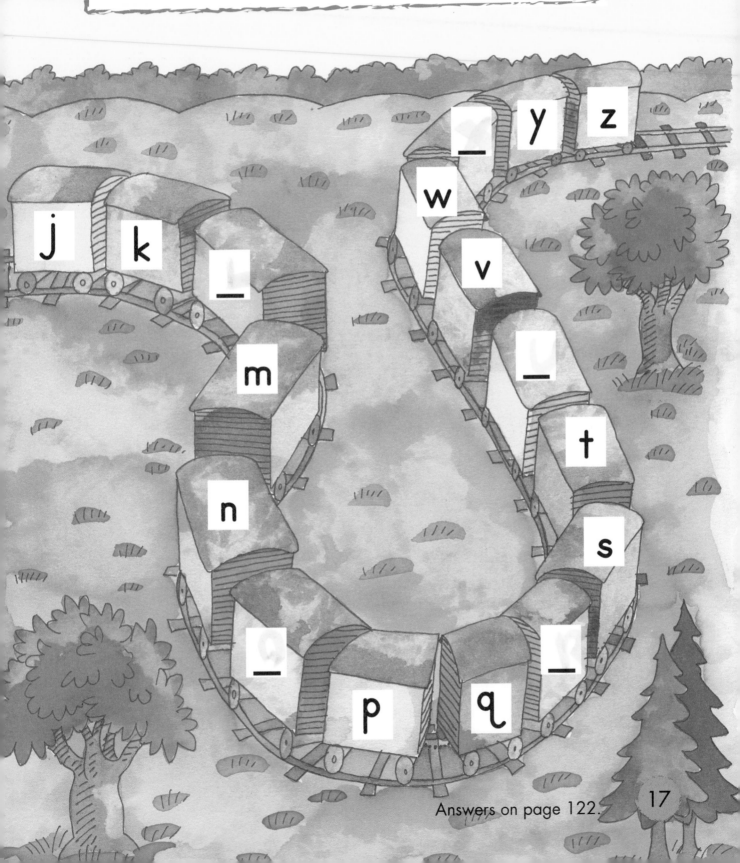

Letter Match

Draw a line from each crayon with an uppercase letter to the scribble with the lowercase letter that matches it. Then color each scribble the same color as the matching crayon.

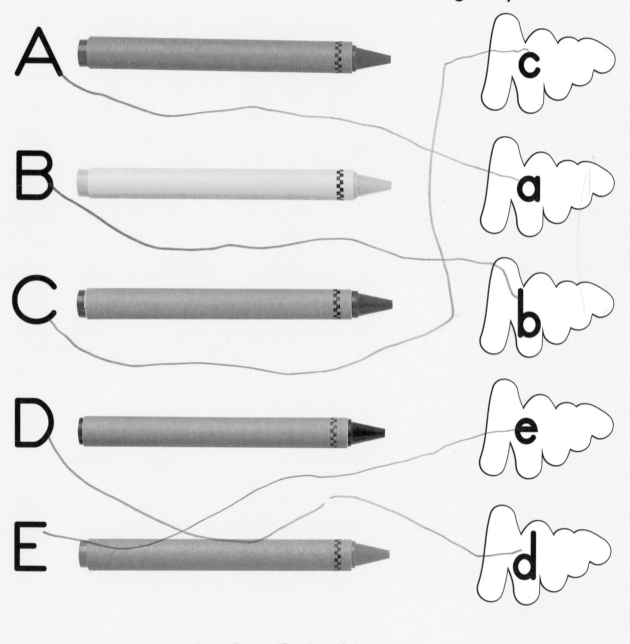

Skill: Matching uppercase letters to lowercase letters Aa–Ee

Answers on page 122.

Mother Match

Help the baby animals find their mothers. Draw a line from each baby with a lowercase letter to the mother with the uppercase letter that matches it.

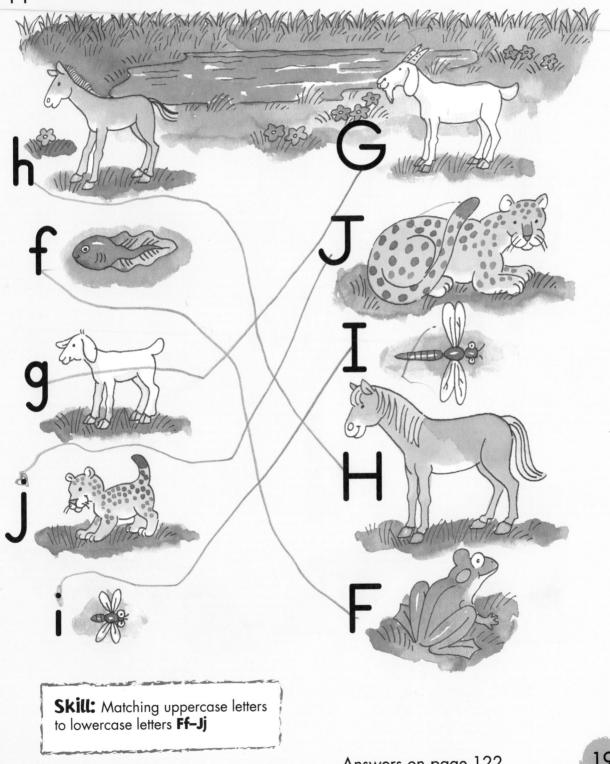

Answers on page 122.

Flower Power

Write the lowercase letter that matches the uppercase letter on each flower petal. As you make your match, cross out the letters on the leaves at the bottom.

Answers on page 122.

Color by Letter

Color each group of matching lowercase and uppercase letters with a different colored crayon or marker. You can choose any color you want. What picture do you see?

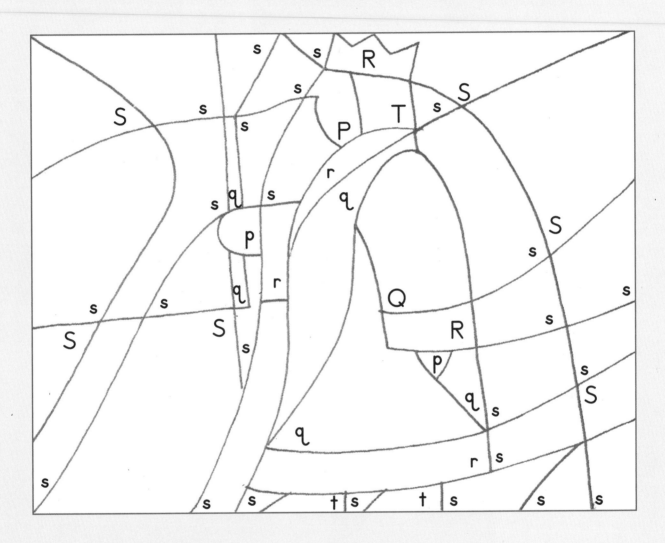

Skill: Matching uppercase letters to lowercase letters **Pp–Tt**

Answers on page 122.

Driving the Alphabet

Write the lowercase letter of the alphabet in the flag to match the uppercase letter on each car. Cross out the lowercase letters in the box as you write them with their uppercase match.

u v w x y z

The Letter Bb

The letter **b** says **b** as in **bear.** Listen to the **b** sounds in this sentence: The big brown bear bounced the blue ball. Below, color in yes or no if the pictures start with the sound of **b.**

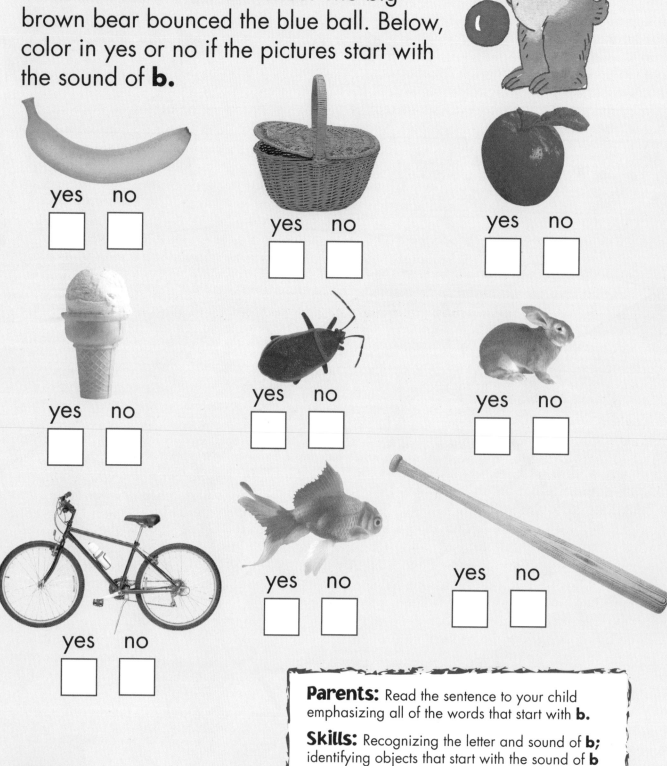

yes   no
☐   ☐

yes   no
☐   ☐

yes   no
☐   ☐

yes   no
☐   ☐

yes   no
☐   ☐

yes   no
☐   ☐

yes   no
☐   ☐

yes   no
☐   ☐

yes   no
☐   ☐

Parents: Read the sentence to your child emphasizing all of the words that start with **b.**

Skills: Recognizing the letter and sound of **b;** identifying objects that start with the sound of **b**

24

Answers on page 122.

The Letter Cc as in Cat

The letter **c** says **c** as in **cat.** This is called the hard **c.** Listen for the hard **c** sound in **cat.** Circle all of the things that start with the sound of hard **c.**

Parents: Look at the picture with your child and emphasize all of the words that start with **c.** Help your child keep track of all the words that start with **c.**

Skills: Recognizing the letter and sound of hard **c;** identifying objects that start with the sound of hard **c**

Answers on page 122.

The Letter Cc as in City

The letter **c** also says **c** as in **city.** This is called the soft **c** sound. Listen for the soft **c** sound in this sentence: Cindy ate cereal in the center of her city. Write the letter **c** under all of the pictures that start with the soft **c.**

```
. . . . . . . . . . .          . . . . . . . . . . .          . . . . . . . . . . .          . . . . . . . . . . .
```

```
. . . . . . . . . . .          . . . . . . . . . . .          . . . . . . . . . . .
```

Parents: Read the sentence with/to your child emphasizing all of the words that start with the sound of soft **c.** Have your child trace over all of the letter **c**'s in the sentence.

Skills: Recognizing the letter and sound of soft **c;** identifying objects that start with the sound of soft **c**

Answers on page 123.

The Letter Dd

The letter **d** says **d** as in **day.** Can you hear the **d** in **day** and **door?** Circle the things that start with the **d** sound.

Skills: Recognizing the letter and sound of **d;** identifying objects that start with the sound of **d**

Answers on page 123.

The Letter Ff

The letter **f** says **f** as in **fish.** Listen for the **f** sound as you say **fish.** Help the fish find his way to the fishbowl by following the path with the pictures that start with **f.** Draw a line through each picture as you go.

Skills: Recognizing the letter and sound of **f;** identifying objects that start with the sound of **f**

Answers on page 123.

The Hard Sound of Gg

The letter **g** says **g** as in **goat.** This sound is called the hard
g. Can you hear the hard **g** sound in this sentence? A goat
gave gum to a girl. What else can the goat give to the girl?
Draw a line from the pictures that begin with the hard **g**
sound to the girl.

Skills: Recognizing the letter and sound of hard **g**;
identifying objects that start with the sound of hard **g**

Answers on page 123.

29

The Soft Sound of Gg

The letter **g** says **g** as in **giraffe.** This sound is called the soft **g.** Listen for the soft **g** sound in the following sentence: Gene, the giraffe, works out in a gym in his new gym clothes. Below, match the pictures to the words with the soft **g** sound.

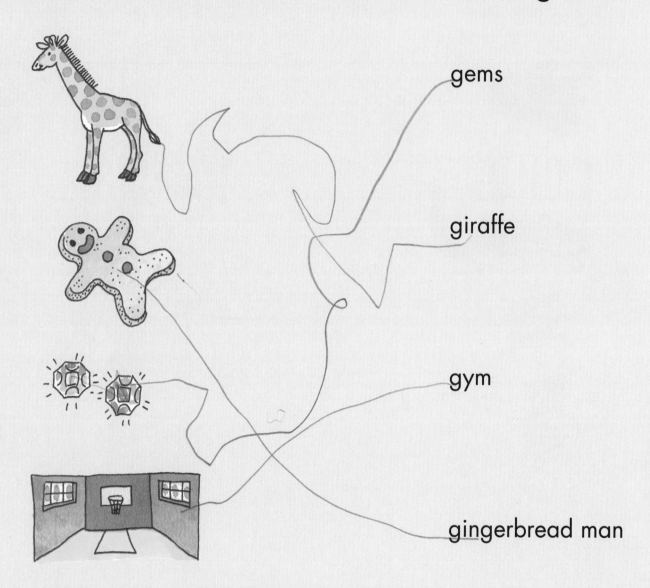

gems

giraffe

gym

gingerbread man

Skills: Recognizing the letter and sound of soft **g**; identifying objects that start with the sound of soft **g**

30

Answers on page 123.

The Letter Hh

The letter **h** says **h** as in **hat**. Write the letter **h** on the blanks to make a word. Practice reading your **h** words.

hamster

hammer

hen

hat

The Letter Jj

The letter **j** says **j** as in **jump.** Can you hear the **j** sounds in **jaguar, jump rope,** and **jungle?** Put all of the pictures that start with the sound of **j** into the jug by drawing lines from the pictures to the jug.

Answers on page 123.

The Letter Kk

The letter **k** says **k** as in **kangaroo.** Listen for the sound of **k** in this sentence: A kangaroo and a kitten tied a key on a kite. How many **k** words do you hear? Circle all of the pictures that start with the **k** sound.

Skills: Recognizing the letter and sound of **k;** identifying objects that start with the sound of **k**

Answers on page 123.

The Letter Ll

The letter **l** says **l** as in **lollipop.** Where do you hear the **l** sound? Circle the **l** before or after the picture to show whether the **l** sound is heard at the beginning or the end of the word.

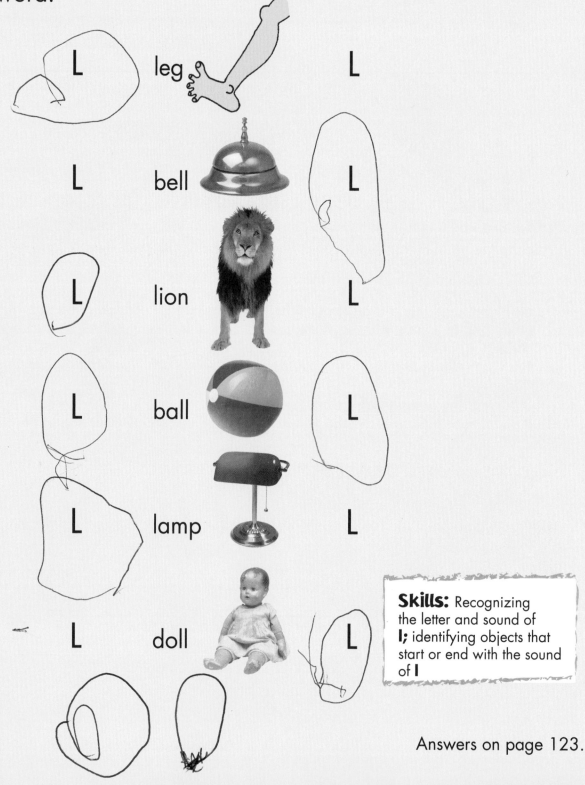

L   leg   L

L   bell   L

L   lion   L

L   ball   L

L   lamp   L

L   doll   L

Skills: Recognizing the letter and sound of **l**; identifying objects that start or end with the sound of **l**

34

Answers on page 123.

The Letter Mm

The letter **m** says **m** as in **monkey.** Listen for the **m** sound in this sentence: The messy monkey had a mop. Draw a line from the monkey to the things that start with the sound of **m.**

Skills: Recognizing the letter and sound of **m;** identifying objects that start with the sound of **m**

Answers on page 123.

The Letter Nn

The letter **n** says **n** as in **nest.** Circle the objects with the **n** sound that the bird has collected in its nest.

Skill: Recognizing the letter and sound of **n**; identifying objects that start with the sound of **n**

Answers on page 123.

The Letter Pp

The letter **p** says **p** as in **pig.** Listen for the **p** sound in this sentence: The pink pig landed perfectly in her purple parachute. Use a pink crayon to color the pictures that start with the **p** sound.

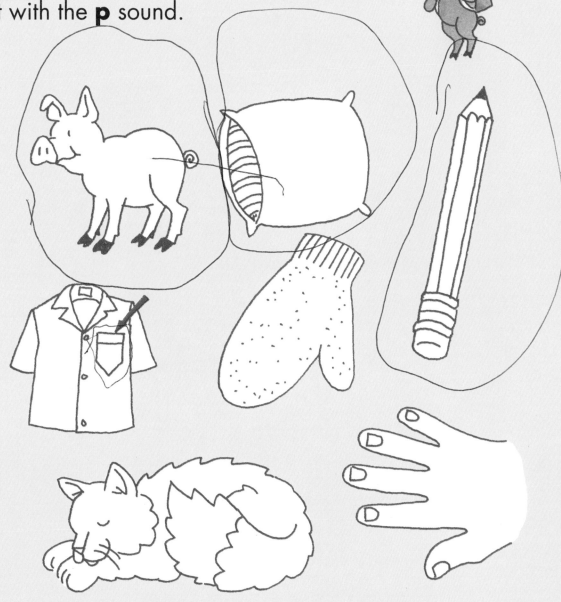

Skills: Recognizing the letter and sound of **p**; identifying objects that start with the sound of **p**

Answers on page 123.

The Letter Qq

The letter **q** says **q** as in **quilt**. **Q** is almost always followed by the letter **u** to make **qu**. Listen for the **q** sounds in this sentence: The queen paid a quarter for a quilt. Circle the word in each row that begins with the sound of **q**.

Answers on page 123.

The Letter Rr

The letter **r** says **r** as in **rainbow.** Listen to the **r** sound in **rainbow.** Write **r** at the beginning of each line to make **r** words that match the pictures.

__ainbow

__abbit

__ain

__ose

__ake

Skills: Recognizing the letter and sound of **r;** identifying objects that start with the sound of **r**

Answers on page 123.

The Letter Ss

The letter **s** says **s** as in **sun.** How many words in the following sentence start with the **s** sound? The seal hangs seven socks in the sun. Circle the **s** before or after the picture to show if you hear the **s** at the beginning or the end of the word.

S   sun   S

S   sock   S

S   bus   S

S   soap   S

S   mouse   S

S   sandwich   S

Skills: Recognizing the letter and sound of **s**; identifying objects that start or end with the sound of **s**

40

Answers on page 123.

The Letter Tt

The letter **t** says **t** as in **tooth.** Listen to the sound that **t** makes in the following sentence: Two turtles took a truck to town. Two turtles are taking a trip in a truck. Choose the **t** objects the turtles will take with them. Draw a line from the pictures that start with the **t** sound to the back of the truck.

Skills: Recognizing the letter and sound of **t;** identifying objects that start with the sound of **t**

Answers on page 123.

The Letter Vv

The letter **v** says the **v** sound as in **vest.** Vikki has lots of things in her room that start with **v.** Circle the items that start with the sound of **v.**

Skills: Recognizing the letter and sound of **v;** identifying objects that start with the sound of **v**

Answers on page 124.

The Letter Ww

The letter **w** says the **w** sound as in **web.** Look at the Wacky Web. Can you find all of the pictures that start with the **w** sound? Draw a line from the spider to the things that begin with the sound of **w.**

Skills: Recognizing the letter and sound of **w;** identifying objects that start with the sound of **w**

Answers on page 124.

The Letter Xx

The letter **x** says **x**, as in **fox**. Listen for the **x** sound in this poem:

> **x** is for **X**-ray
>
> **x** is in fo**x**
>
> **x** is for **X**'s
>
> on the bo**x**.

Write an **x** at the beginning or end of the words to match the pictures. Say the words and listen for the **x** sound.

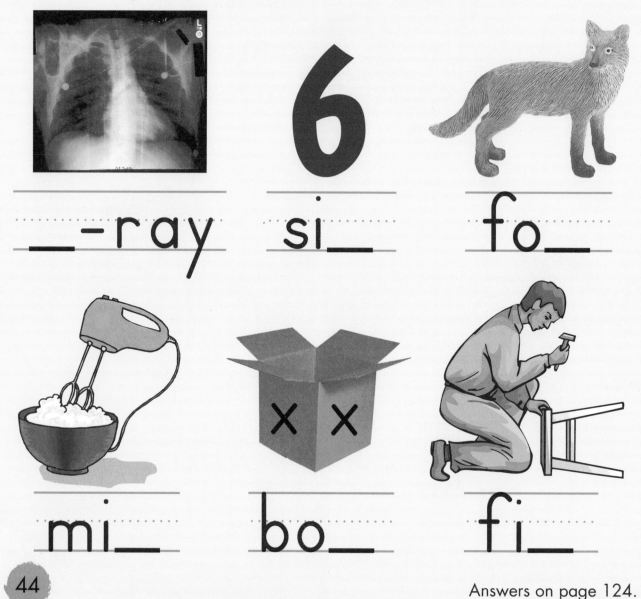

___-ray   si___   fo___

mi___   bo___   fi___

Answers on page 124.

The Letter Yy

The letter **y** says **y** as in **yarn.** Listen to all of the words that make the **y** sound in this sentence: The yak rolled his yellow yo-yo. The yak needs help. Which string leads to the yellow yo-yo? Follow the correct string, and write the number of the string here ____.

1
2
3

> **Skills:** Recognizing the letter and sound of **y;** identifying objects that start with the sound of **y**

Answer on page 124.

45

The Letter Zz

The letter **z** says **z** as in **zoo.** Can you find the hidden things in this picture that begin with the **z** sound? Circle them when you find them.

Answers on page 124.

Wing It!

Match the uppercase letter on each butterfly to its lowercase partner by coloring each pair of butterflies the same color. Practice writing the uppercase and lowercase letters in the spaces provided.

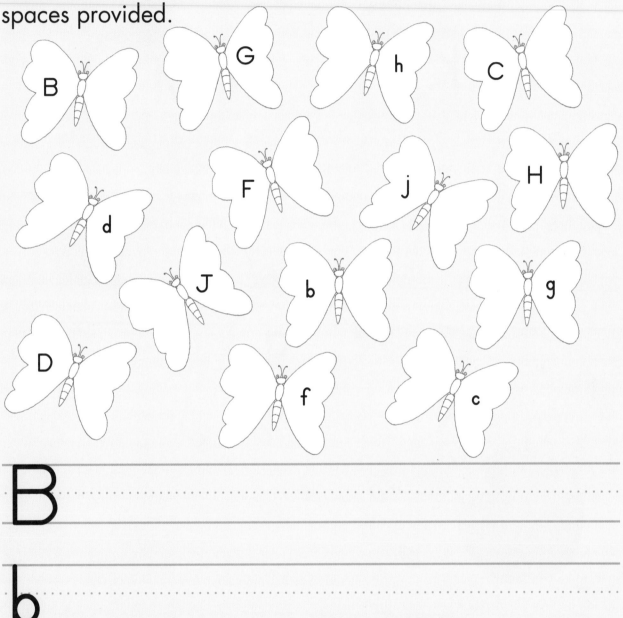

B

b

Parents: Guide your child in forming the letters. If you need to, write the letters in one color, and let your child trace them in another color.

Skill: Learning how to write and form the letters **Bb, Cc, Dd, Ff, Gg, Hh, Jj**

Answers on page 124.

Writing Is Fun!

Write the missing upper- and lowercase letters in your best handwriting on each part of the caterpillar.

Parents: Help your child write the letters with pencil, crayons, or colored pencils. You may want to write the letters first in one color and let your child trace them in another color.

Skill: Learning how to write and form the letters **Kk, Ll, Mm, Nn, Pp, Qq, Rr**

Answers on page 124.

Follow the Letters

Fill in the missing upper- or lowercase letters to help lead the boy to his lost dog.

Skill: Learning how to write and form the letters Ss, Tt, Vv, Ww, Xx, Yy, Zz

Answers on page 124.

Short Vowel Aa

A is a vowel. Vowels have two sounds, short and long. The short vowel **a** sounds like the **a** you hear in the word **cat.** Fill in the missing **a** to complete the words that have the short vowel sound of **a.** Use the pictures to help you read the word.

A also is used at the beginning of some words. Write an **a** at the beginning of each word to make words that start with the short **a** sound.

__pple

__nimal

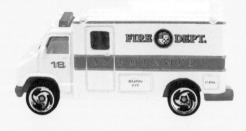

__mbulance

__nt

__lligator

Skill: Recognizing the short sound of the vowel/letter **a**

Short Vowel Ee

E is a vowel. Vowels have two sounds, short and long. The short vowel **e** sounds like the **e** you hear in the middle of the word **bed** and at the beginning of the word **egg.** Circle the pictures that have the short **e** sound in them.

Fill in the missing **e** to make words that have the short **e** sound. Use the pictures to help you.

_gg

b_d

b_ll

_lephant

Answers on page 124.

Short Vowel Ii

The letter **i** is a vowel. Vowels have two sounds, short and long. The short vowel **i** sounds like the **i** you hear in the middle of the word **pig** and at the beginning of the word **igloo.** Circle the word with the short **i** sound that matches the picture. Next, write the word on the line under the picture.

wig   **big**   **lip**   **pig**   **six**   **hill**

Write an **i** at the beginning of each word to make words that start with the short **i** sound.

_gloo   _guana

Skill: Recognizing the short sound of the vowel/letter **i**

Answers on page 124.

Short Vowel Oo

The letter **o** is a vowel. Vowels have two sounds, short and long. The short vowel **o** sounds like the **o** you hear in the middle of the word **mop** and at the beginning of the word **octopus.** The octopus only wants to hold objects with the short **o** sound! Circle all the things that have the short **o** sound. Cross out the things that do not.

Skill: Recognizing the short sound of the vowel/letter **o**

Answers on page 124.

55

Short Vowel Uu

The letter **u** is a vowel. Vowels have two sounds, short and long. The short vowel **u** sounds like the **u** you hear in the middle of the word **sun** and at the beginning of the word **up.** Fill in the missing letters to make words with the short **u** sound.

___ u ___

___ u ___

___ u ___

___ u ___

Skill: Recognizing the short sound of the vowel/letter **u**

Answers on page 124.

Long Vowel Aa

The long vowel **a** sounds like the **a** you hear in the word **game.** Connect the pictures with the long **a** sound by drawing a line from the first picture with the long **a** sound at the Start to the next, and then the next. See if you can make it to the Finish to win the game!

Skill: Recognizing the long sound of the vowel/letter **a**

Answers on page 124.

Long Vowel Ee

The long vowel **e** sounds like the **e** you hear in the word **eagle.** The long **e** sound is sometimes written with **ee** or **ea.** Draw a line from the picture to the word that matches it.

leaf

bee

seal

cheese

Skills: Recognizing the long sound of the vowel/letter **e**

58

Answers on page 125.

Long Vowel Ii

The long vowel **i** sounds like the **i** in the word **kite.** Fill in the missing **i** in the words on the kites. Draw strings from the kites to the matching pictures with the long **i** sound.

b_ke

t_re

_ce cream

n_ne

Answers on page 125.

Long Vowel Oo

The long vowel **o** sounds like the **o** in the word **boat.** Circle the things in the boat that have the long **o** sound. Cross out those that do not.

Skill: Recognizing the long sound of the vowel/letter **o**

Answers on page 125.

Long Vowel Uu

The long vowel **u** sounds like the **u** in the word **cube.** Make an X through the pictures with the long **u** sound. Did you get a tic-tac-toe?

Fill in the missing **u** to make a word that has the long **u** sound.

m__sic

Skill: Recognizing the long sound of the vowel/letter **u**

Answers on page 125.

Handy Dandy Words: the, of, and

Three of the Handy Dandy Words are **the, of, and.** You will see these words often when you are reading. Read the sentence, and find the Handy Dandy Word. Copy it onto the line. Practice reading your words every day!

The  plays with a  .

....

A  has a  of  .

....

My  and my  are red.

....

My 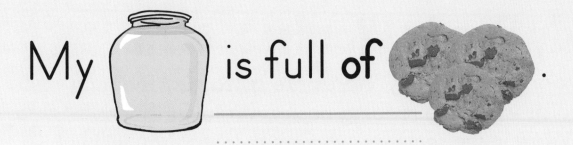 is full **of** .

_____

. . . .

_____

A  **and** a live at a zoo.

_____

. . . .

_____

 **The** is tall.

_____

. . . .

_____

Parents: The Handy Dandy Words occur over and over in written English. Teaching your child to read these words will enable them to read more fluently.

Skill: Recognizing the high-frequency words **the, of, and**

Handy Dandy Words: a, to, in

Three more Handy Dandy Words are **a, to, in.** Learning these words will make reading easier. Write the Handy Dandy Word in the sentence where it belongs. You will use each word only once!

The girl makes _____ snowman.

The dog is _____ the tub.

The kids are going _____ school.

a to in

Answers on page 125.

Handy Dandy Words: is, you, that, it

The Handy Dandy Words **is, you, that, it** are also great to know! Read the poem and find the Handy Dandy Words. Circle them, and then write them in the blank spaces provided.

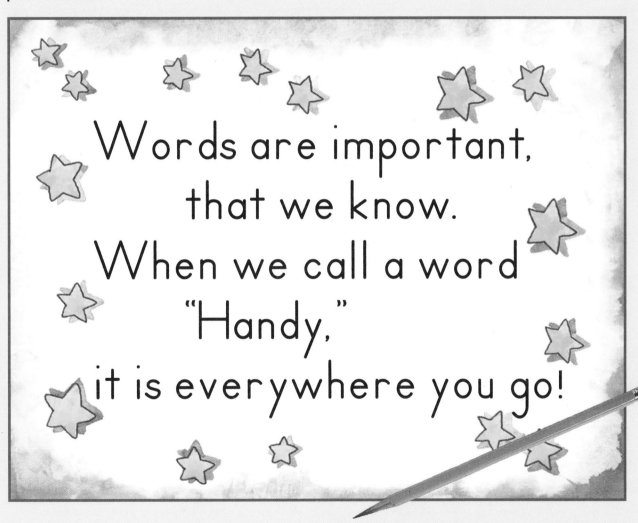

Words are important,
that we know.
When we call a word
"Handy,"
it is everywhere you go!

_____ _____ _____ _____

Play Ball!

The word **baseball** starts with the sound of the letter **b.** Fill in the missing **b** at the beginning of each word. Then circle all the things that start with the sound of the letter **b.**

_oy

_at

_all

Parents: Have your child write the letter **b** in each of the spaces to help them form words. Then name the pictures with them.

Skill: Recognizing initial consonants in words that start with the **b** sound

66

Answers on page 125.

Pack the Car!

The word **car** starts with the letter **c.** In the word **car,** the **c** says the hard **c** sound. Carrie can only pack the car with things that start with the letter **c** and have the hard **c** sound. Circle the things she should pack, and cross out those she shouldn't. Write the letter **c** in the space at the beginning of each word. Try to read the words!

_up

_oat

_an

_andy

Skill: Recognizing initial consonants in words that start with the hard **c** sound

Answers on page 125.

City Circus

The words **circus** and **city** start with the letter **c.** In these words, the **c** says the soft sound of **c.** Make your way from the city to the circus by following the path with the pictures that begin with the soft **c** sound. Write the letter **c** in the spaces to complete the words.

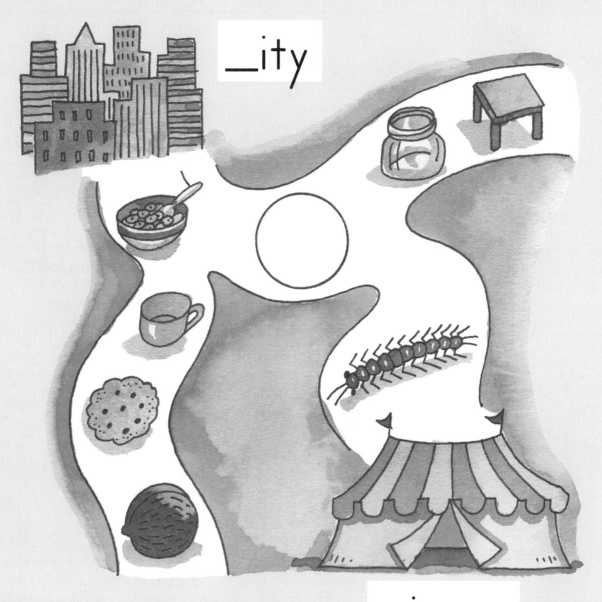

_ity

_ircus

Skill: Recognizing initial consonants in words that start with the soft **c** sound

Answers on page 125.

Detective Dog

The word **dog** stars with the sound of the letter **d.** Fill in the missing **d** to complete each word.

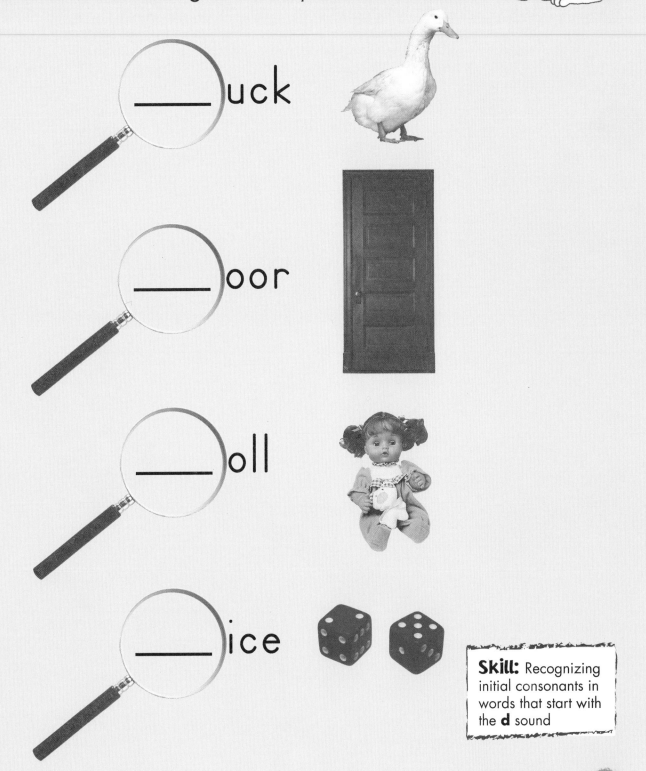

_____uck

_____oor

_____oll

_____ice

Answers on page 125.

69

Fantastic Fish

The word **fish** starts with the sound of the letter **f.** Draw a line from the fishing pole to the objects that begin with the sound of the letter **f.** Write the missing **f** to complete the words. Look at the pictures near the words to help you.

_lippers

_an

_ork

_ish

_our

Answers on page 125. 71

Go for the Gold

The word **gold** starts with the letter **g.** In the word **gold,** the **g** says the hard **g** sound. Grace can only kick the soccer balls with pictures that start with the hard **g** sound. Color the soccer balls with pictures that start with the hard **g** sound. Write the missing **g** in each space.

Skill: Recognizing initial consonants in words that start with the hard **g** sound

_rapes

_old

Answers on page 125.

Soft Gg Sound

The word **giant** starts with the letter **g.** In the word **giant,** the **g** says the soft **g** sound. Name each picture and listen for the soft **g** sound. Write the letter **g** in each of the spaces below to complete the words.

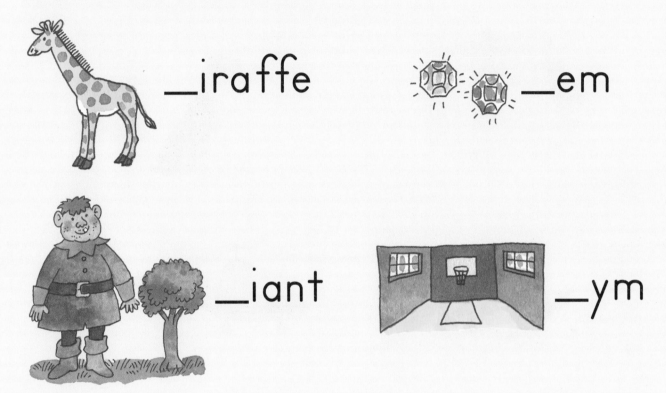

_iraffe

_em

_iant

_ym

_erbil

Skill: Recognizing initial consonants in words that start with the soft **g** sound

Answers on page 125.

Helping Hands

The word **hand** starts with the sound of the letter **h.** Circle each picture that begins with the **h** sound and cross out each picture that does not.

Answers on page 126.

Juggling Jj's

The word **jar** starts with the sound of the letter **j**. Circle the pictures that start with the sound of the letter **j**. At the bottom, practice writing the **j** to make **j** words.

_ump rope

_ellybeans

Skill: Recognizing initial consonants in words that start with the **j** sound

Answers on page 126.

Doors Galore!

The word **key** starts with the sound of the letter **k.** Kevin's key can only unlock the doors with things that begin with the sound of the letter **k.** Draw a line from Kevin's key to the doors with the correct pictures, then write the beginning letter **k** to make **k** words.

Skill: Recognizing initial consonants in words that start with the **k** sound

_ettle

_angaroo

_ing

76

Answers on page 126.

Lots of Locks!

The word **lock** starts with the sound of the letter **l.** Draw a line from the pictures that start with the sound of **l** to the lock in the center of the page. Practice writing **l**'s to finish the words that start with **l.** Use the pictures to help you read the words.

__ion

__ips

__eg

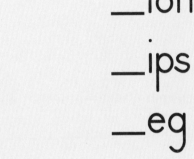

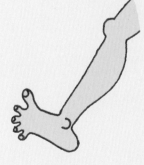

Skill: Recognizing initial consonants in words that start with the **l** sound

Answers on page 126.

Marvelous Mittens

The word **mitten** starts with the sound of the letter **m.**

Help the mittens find their matches! Follow each mitten's string to lead it to its partner. Practice writing the letter **m** on the mittens and fill in the missing **m** at the bottom of the page to make words that begin with the **m** sound.

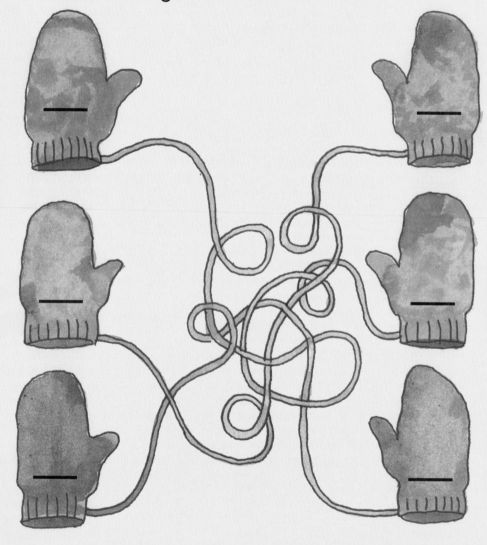

_itten   _atch

Skill: Recognizing initial consonants in words that start with the **m** sound

Answers on page 126.

Read All About It!

The word **newspaper** starts with the sound of the letter **n.** Look at the pictures in the newspaper and color the pictures that begin with the sound of the letter **n.** Then fill in the missing **n** to complete the words. Look at the pictures for help.

 __est

 __ickel

Answers on page 126.

Prized Pigs!

The word **pig** starts with the sound of the letter **p.** Fill in the missing **p** to complete the word.

_ig

The black and white pig won the contest. Help him circle a prize that begins with the **p** sound.

The pink pig came in second. She also wants the prize that begins with the **p** sound. Circle the prize that she should choose.

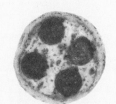

The white pig got third place. He won a prize that begins with the **p** sound too. Circle the prize that he won.

> **Skill:** Recognizing initial consonants in words that begin with the **p** sound

Answers on page 126.

Words that Start with Qq

The word **quilt** starts with the letter **q.** The letter **q** is almost always paired with **u.** Fill in the missing **qu** to complete words that have the sound of the letter **q.** Then circle the pictures that match the words.

__een   __arter   __ilt

Skill: Recognizing initial consonants in words that begin with the **q** sound

Answers on page 126.

Words that Start with Rr

The word **rabbit** starts with the sound of the letter **r.** Write the missing **r** to make words that begin with the sound of the letter **r.** Read the words, then draw lines from the words to the pictures that match them.

_ose

_abbit

_ing

_ake

_ug

Answers on page 126.

Hungry Snake!

The word **snake** starts with the sound of the letter **s.** The snake has swallowed some objects. Color in the pictures that begin with the sound of the letter **s.** Fill in the missing **s** to complete the word.

_nake

Skill: Recognizing initial consonants in words that begin with the **s** sound

Answers on page 126.

Terrific Turtles!

The word **turtle** starts with the sound of the letter **t.** Help the turtles choose the picture that begins with the sound of **t** in each column by circling it. At the bottom of each column, write the name of the picture you circled. Use the word bank at the bottom to help you write the words.

Skill: Recognizing initial consonants in words that begin with the **t** sound

tire tent ten tie

Answers on page 126.

Words that Start with Vv

The word **van** starts with the sound of the letter **v.** The van can only carry objects that start with the letter **v.** Write the letter **v** to complete the word. Then, load the van with the correct items: Draw lines to the van from the pictures that begin with the letter **v.**

__an

Skill: Recognizing initial consonants in words that begin with the **v** sound

Answers on page 126.

Wagons and Wheelbarrows!

The words **wagon** and **wheelbarrow** start with the letter **w.** Circle the word that matches the object in the wagon or wheelbarrow. Then write the word you circled on the line below it.

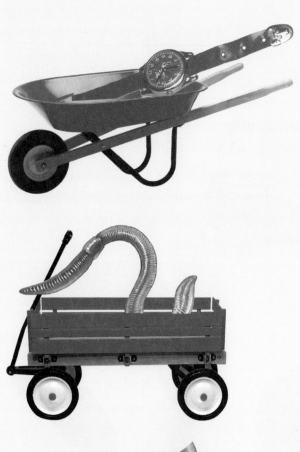

wet

watch

wild

_____

....

_____

what

worm

west

_____

....

_____

when

watermelon

wept

_____

....

_____

86

walk

wolf

wax

_____

. . . .

_____

wig

win

wet

_____

. . . .

_____

wood

whale

we

_____

. . . .

_____

Skill: Recognizing initial consonants in words that begin with the **w** sound

Answers on page 126.

Words that Start with Yy

The word **yak** starts with the sound of the letter **y.** Say the name of each picture and read the words below it. Circle the word that matches the picture and write the word on the line.

yuck   yarn

_____

. . . .

_____

yard   yak

_____

. . . .

_____

yes   yellow

_____

. . . .

_____

yo-yo   you

_____

. . . .

_____

Skill: Recognizing initial consonants in words that begin with the **y** sound

88

Answers on page 126.

Words that Start with Zz

The word **zebra** starts with the sound of the letter **z.** Write the correct word that starts with the sound of the letter **z** below each picture. Use the word bank to help you write the words. Cross out the words as you use them.

Skill: Recognizing initial consonants in words that begin with the **z** sound

zebra zero zipper zigzag

Answers on page 126.

Rhyme Time

Rhyming words are words that end with the same sound. When you say them, the words sound the same, so they **rhyme.** For example, **fox** and **socks** are rhyming words. **Fox** and **socks** rhyme. Draw a line from the picture on the left to the picture that rhymes on the right.

Parents: You can play rhyming games with your child. Say a word and then ask your child to think of a word that rhymes with the word you said.

Skill: Identifying rhyming words by sound

90

Answers on page 127.

Find a Rhyme

It is fun to think up words to rhyme with other words! Read the words under the pictures in each row. Color the two pictures that have rhyming words.

top   bell   mop

pig   wig   bag

rug   rat   hat

Skill: Identifying rhyming words in print

Answers on page 127.

Rhyme Me a Poem!

Poems and songs often have rhyming words in them. It is
fun to listen for rhyming words. Underline all of the rhyming
words you can hear in this poem.

I have a cat,

who sits on a mat.

He ate cookies and cake,

in the sand by the lake.

He liked to lay in the sun,

now he's so big, he can't even run.

Now, draw a line from the picture on the left to the picture that rhymes with it on the right.

Skill: Identifying rhyming words in poems

Answers on page 127.

Word Families

Groups of words that have the same ending are called **word families.** Use a red crayon to color all of the shirts from the **-at** word family, and a blue crayon to color all of the shirts from the **-an** word family.

Parents: You can write these words on index cards and have your child group the words that belong in the same word family.

Skill: Recognizing word families for words that end with **-an** and **-at**

Answers on page 127.

Word Family Farm

Groups of words that end with **-ed** and **-en** are said to belong in the **-ed** or **-en** word family. Draw lines from the animals with **-ed** endings to the **-ed** word family barn. Draw lines from the animals with **-en** endings to the **-en** word family barn.

Skill: Recognizing word families for words that end with **-ed** and **-en**

Answers on page 127.

95

Writing Word Families

Word family endings also include **-ub** and **-ug.** Write either the **-ub** or the **-ug** word family ending to form words that match the pictures.

c_ _

s_ _

t_ _

b_ _

m_ _

j_ _

Skill: Recognizing word families for words that end with **-ub** and **-ug**

Answers on page 127.

Word Family Match-Up

When you change a letter at the beginning of **-an** words, you can make a new word. Draw a line from the **-an** word to the correct picture.

can

man

pan

van

Answers on page 127.

Word Family Recess!

When you change a letter at the beginning of **-ell** words, you can make a new word. Fill in the missing **-ell** to complete the word. Try to read the words. Use the pictures to help you.

Skill: Recognizing the word family for words that end with **-ell**

b_ _ _

y_ _ _

sh_ _ _ _

f_ _ _

Answers on page 127.

Word Switch

Changing the first letters in words is so much fun! Add a first letter from the box to form the **-ill** word that matches the picture. You will use each letter only once.

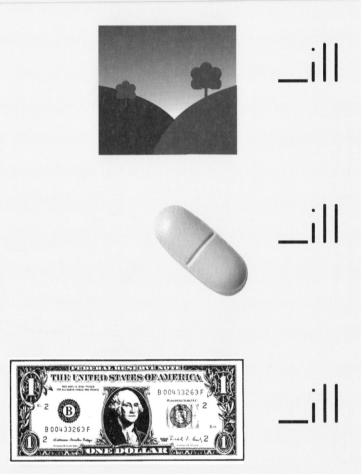

_ill

_ill

_ill

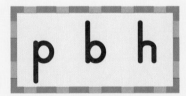

p   b   h

Skill: Changing the initial consonant for words in the **-ill** word family

Answers on page 127.

Make Mine Match

If you change the first letter of a word to an uppercase letter, it is still the same word. For example, if the word **run** is changed to **Run,** it is still the same word! Color each pair of socks that have matching words with a different colored crayon or marker. You can choose any color you want.

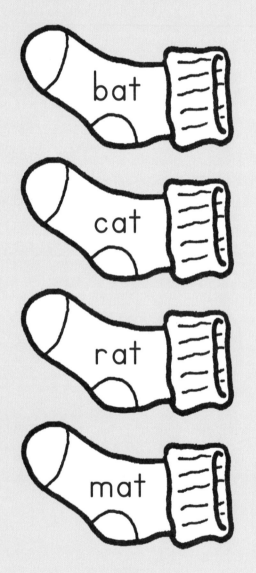

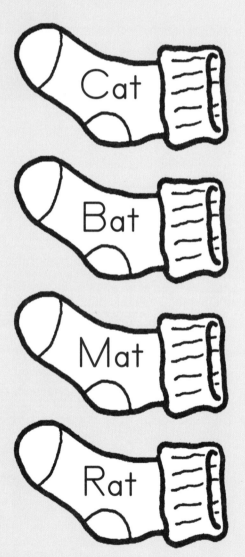

Answers on page 127.

Tub Time

Most consonants usually stand for the same sound at the end of a word as at the beginning of a word. The letter **b** usually says the same sound at both the beginning and end of words. You can hear this sound at the end of the word **tub.** Circle the pictures that end with the sound of **b.**

Parents: You can have your child name items in your home and listen to the sounds at the end of words. He or she can also try to find items with the same ending sounds.

Skill: Recognizing the sound usually represented by the letter **b** at the end of a word

Birds of a Feather

The letter **d** will usually stand for the same sound at the end of a word as it does at the beginning of a word. You can hear this sound at the end of the word **bird.** Use a yellow crayon to color the birds that have words ending with the **d** sound.

Skill: Recognizing the sound usually represented by the letter **d** at the end of a word

Answers on page 127.

Moving Day

At the end of a word, the letter **g** usually says the sound you hear at the end of the word **bug.** Circle the bugs that are carrying pictures that end with the **g** sound. At the bottom, fill in the missing **g** to make words that end with the **g** sound.

Skill: Recognizing the sound usually represented by the letter **g** at the end of a word

ba__

bu__

Answers on page 127.

Toy Store

At the end of a word, the letter **k** usually says the sound you hear at the end of the word **clock.** When there is a **-ck** at the end of a word, the **c** and **k** stay together to say a single sound. Circle all of the pictures that end in the **k** sound.

At the end of a word, the letter **l** or letters **ll** usually say the sound you hear at the end of the word **mail** or **ball**. Add **-l** or **-ll** to the end of each word to complete it.

pai__

sai__

nai__

ba____

do____

Skill: Recognizing the sound usually represented by the letter **l** at the end of a word

106

Answers on page 128.

In the Diner

At the end of a word, the letter **p** usually says the sound you hear at the end of the word **cup.** Draw a line from the letter **p** that the server is carrying to the words that end in the **p** sound. At the bottom, fill in the missing **p** to form two words that end in the **p** sound. Use the pictures to help you.

 ma__

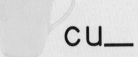 cu__

Skill: Recognizing the sound usually represented by the letter **p** at the end of a word

Answers on page 128.

Give Me an "R"!

At the end of a word, the letter **r** usually says the sound you hear at the end of the word **cheer.** Add the missing **r** to make words that end with the sound of **r.** Draw a line from each cheerleader's sign to the correct picture.

Answers on page 128.

Best Dressed

At the end of a word, the letter **s** usually says the sound that you hear at the end of the word **dress.** Tess needs a new dress! Help her choose by coloring in the dresses with pictures that end in the **s** sound. Write the words for the pictures that end in **s** at the bottom.

_____   _____   _____
. . . .
_____   _____   _____

Answers on page 128.

Follow the Trail

At the end of a word, the letter **t** usually says the sound you hear at the end of the words **cat** and **rat.** The cat is trying to find the rat. Draw a line through the pictures that end with the sound of **t** to lead the cat to it!

Skill: Recognizing the sound usually represented by the letter **t** at the end of a word

Answers on page 128.

Fox in Box

The letter **x** at the end of a word usually makes a sound almost like a **k** and **s** sound put together. You can hear it at the end of words like **fox** and **box.** Which words end with the sound of **x**? Circle all of the pictures ending with the sound of **x** that you find in the boxes.

Skill: Recognizing the sound usually represented by the letter **x** at the end of a word

Answers on page 128.

Change a Word

You can sometimes change the last letter of a word to make a new word. Choose a different ending letter to make a new word that matches the picture. Write the new word on the line.

hut (g, m) _____

hot (p, g) _____

pad (l, n) _____

mat (n, d) _____

Skill: Substituting final consonants

114

Answers on page 128.

Building Words

When you change the last letter of a word, it changes the way you pronounce the word out loud. Cross out the final letter and add the new letter beside it to make a new word. Now write the word you just made. Circle the picture that shows the new word.

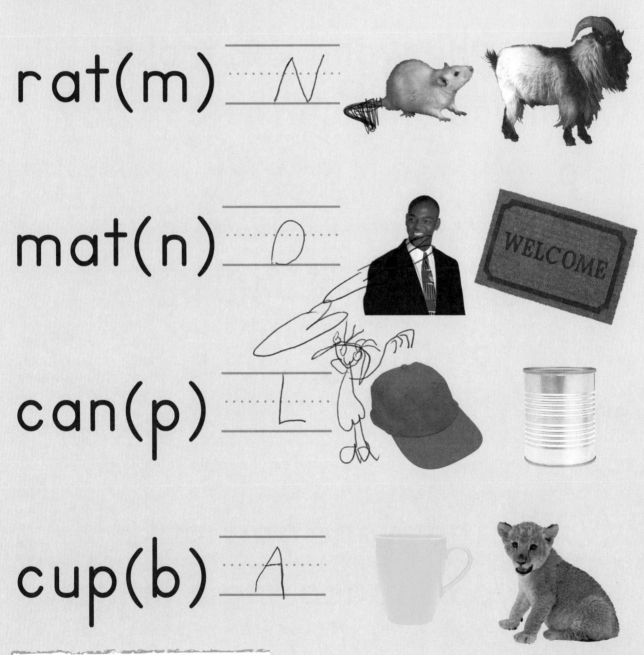

rat(m) _____ N

mat(n) _____ D

can(p) _____ L

cup(b) _____ A

Skills: Substituting final consonants; identifying pictures

Answers on page 128.

What's the Word?

As you already know, you can sometimes change the first letter of a word to make a new word. Look at the words below and follow the directions. Write the new word in the space beside each sentence.

Write the word you make when you change the **d** in **day** to **p**. TOP

Write the word you make when you change the **s** in **set** to **j**. _____

Write the word you make when you change the **z** in **zip** to **l**. _____

Write the word you make when you change the **h** in **hog** to **d**. ....

Write the word you make when you change the **h** in **hut** to **n**. ....

Write the word you make when you change the **m** in **man** to **c**. ....

Answers on page 128.

Vowel Prowl

You can also make new words by changing the vowel sound in the middle of a word. Change the middle vowels in each word to make a new word that matches the picture. You will use the vowels **a, e, i, o,** and **u.** You will use each vowel only one time.

bad

bell

pen

big

pet

Skill: Changing medial vowels to make new words

Answers on page 128.

What's the Ending?

You can sometimes make new words by changing the last letter of a word. Look at the word on the left. Change the ending letter of each word to the new letter in parentheses to make a new word. Draw a line from each new word to its picture, then write the new word on the line.

had(t)

pet(n)

run(g)

bad(t)

Skill: Changing final consonants to make new words

Answers on page 128.

Good Work!

Word Fun

now this book is almost done.

And I have had lots of fun.

Knowing my letters makes me feel smart.

And with my reading, I'm off to a good start.

Each day I will look all around me,

at all the words there are to see.

I will listen to the letters made when I say each word.

I will listen for all of the sounds I have heard.

I will think about letters on everything I see.

I'm a Word Detective—yippee!

Parents: Read the poem to your child, emphasizing the rhyming words. Then guide your child in writing his or her first and last names in the handwriting space on the next page.

Skill: Understanding that knowing letters and sounds contributes to success in reading

sat hat

bat sun

run fun

Congratulations

_____

is a

Word Detective!

Keep up the good work!

Answer Pages

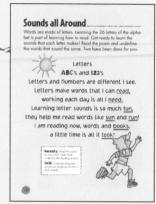

page 10

page 12   page 13

page 16   page 17

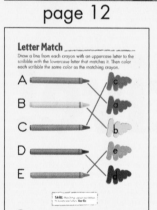

page 18

page 19

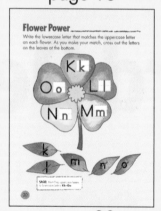

page 20

page 21

page 22   page 23

page 24   page 25

122

The Letter Cc as in City
The letter c also says c as in city. This is called the soft c sound. Listen for the soft c sound in this sentence: Cindy ate cereal in the center of her city.
Write the letter c under all of the pictures that start with the soft c.

page 26

The Letter Dd
The letter d says d as in dog and duck? Can you hear the d in dog and duck?
Circle the pictures that start with the d sound.

page 27

The Letter Ff
The letter f says f as in fish. Listen for the f sound as you say fish.
Help the fish find his way to the fish bowl by circling all the pictures that start with f.

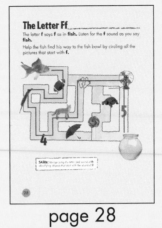

page 28

The Hard Sound of Gg
The letter g says g as in goat. This sound is called the hard g. Can you hear the sound of g in this sentence? A goat gave gum to a girl.
What else can the goat give to the girl? Draw a line from the pictures that begin with the hard g sound to the girl.

page 29

The Soft Sound of Gg
The letter g says g as in giraffe. This sound is called the soft g. Listen for the g sound in the following sentence. Gene, the giraffe, works out in a gym in his new gym clothes.
Below, match the g words with the pictures.

page 30

The Letter Hh
The letter h says h as in hat. Write the letter h on the blanks to make a word. Practice reading your h words.

hamster
hammer
hen
hat

page 31

The Letter Jj
The letter j says j as in jump. Can you hear the j sounds in jaguar, jump rope, and jungle?
Put all of the pictures that start with the sound of j into the jug by drawing lines from the pictures to the jug.

page 32

The Letter Kk
The letter k says k as in kangaroo. Listen for the sound of k in this sentence.
A kangaroo and a kitten tied a key on a kite. How many k words do you hear?
Circle all of the pictures that start with the k sound.

page 33

The Letter Ll
The letter l says l as in lollipop. Where do you hear the l sound? Circle the l before or after the picture to show whether the l sound is heard at the beginning or the end of the word.

page 34

The Letter Mm
The letter m says m as in monkey. Listen for the m sound in this sentence: The messy monkey had a mop.
Draw a line from the monkey to the pictures that start with the sound of m.

page 35

The Letter Nn
The letter n says n as in nest. Circle the n objects that the bird has collected in its nest.

page 36

The Letter Pp
The letter p says p as in pig. Listen for the p sound in this sentence: The pink pig landed perfectly in her purple parachute.
Use a pink crayon to color the pictures that start with the letter p.

page 37

The Letter Qq
The letter q says q as in quilt. Q is almost always followed by the letter u to make qu. Listen for the q sounds in this sentence: The queen paid a quarter for a quilt.
Circle the word in each row that begins with q.

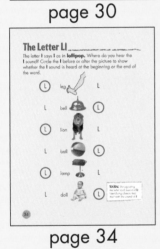

page 38

The Letter Rr
The letter r says r as in rainbow. Listen to the r sound in rainbow.
Write r at the beginning of all the words to make r words that match the pictures.

rainbow
rabbit
rain
rose
rake

page 39

The Letter Ss
The letter s says s as in sun. How many words do you hear that start with the s sound? The squirrel hangs seven socks in the sun.
Circle the s before or after the picture to show if you hear the s at the beginning or the end of the word.

page 40

The Letter Tt
The letter t says t as in tooth. Listen to the sound that t makes in the following sentence: Two turtles took a trip in a truck.
Two turtles are taking a trip in a truck. Choose the t objects the turtles will take with them. Draw a line from the pictures that start with t to the back of the truck.

page 41

123

The Letter Vv
The letter **v** says the **v** sound as in **vest**. Vikki has lots of things in her room that start with **v**. Circle the items that start with the sound of **v** in her room.

SKILL: Recognizing the letter and sound of **v**; identifying objects that start with the sound of **v**.

page 42

The Letter Ww
The letter **w** says the **w** sound as in **web**. Look at the Wacky Web. Can you find all of the pictures that start with **w**? Draw a line from the spider to the pictures that begin with **w**.

SKILL: Recognizing the letter and sound of **w**; identifying objects that start with the sound of **w**.

page 43

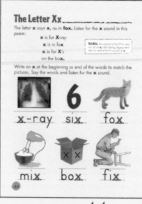
The Letter Xx
The letter **x** says **x**, as in **fox**. Listen for the **x** sound in this poem:

x is for **X**-ray
x is in **fox**
x is for **X**'s
on the box.

Write an **x** at the beginning or end of the words to match the pictures. Say the words and listen for the **x** sound.

x-ray   **6** six   fox

mix   box   fix

page 44

The Letter Yy
The letter **y** says **y** as in **yarn**. Listen to all of the words that make the **y** sound in this sentence: The yak rolled his yellow yo-yo.

The yak needs help—which string leads to the yellow yo-yo? Follow the correct string, and write the number of the string here ___.

SKILL: Recognizing the letter and sound of **y**; identifying objects that start with the sound of **y**.

page 45

The Letter Zz
The letter **z** says **z** as in **zebra**. Can you find the hidden things in this picture that begin with the **z** sound as in the word **zoo**? Circle them once you find them.

SKILL: Recognizing the letter and sound of **z**; identifying objects that start with the sound of **z**.

page 46

Wing It!
Match the uppercase letter on each butterfly to its lowercase partner by coloring each pair of butterflies the same color. Practice writing the uppercase and lowercase letters in the spaces provided.

B C D F J H
b c d f j h

Parents: Guide your child in forming the letters, if you need to, write the spaces you color and let your child trace them in another color.
SKILL: Learning how to write and form the letters Bb, Cc, Dd, Ff, Gg, Hh, Jj.

page 47

Writing Is Fun!
Write the missing upper- and lowercase letters in your best handwriting on each part of the caterpillar.

Kk Ll Mm
Nn
Qq Pp
Rr

Parents: Help your child write the letters with pencil, crayons, or colored pencils.
SKILL: Learning how to write and form the letters Kk, Ll, Mm, Nn, Pp, Qq, Rr.

page 48

Follow the Letters
Fill in the missing upper- or lowercase letters to help lead the boy to his lost dog.

Yy
Xx   Zz
Ww
Ss   Vv
Tt

SKILL: Learning how to write and form the letters Ss, Tt, Vv, Ww, Xx, Yy, Zz.

page 49

Short Vowel Aa
A is a vowel. Vowels have two sounds, short and long. The short vowel **a** sounds like the **a** you hear in the word **cat**. Fill in the missing **a** to complete the words that have the short vowel sound of **a**. Use the pictures to help you read the word.

m a p / P a n
c a n
m a n
h a t
b a t

page 50

A also is used at the beginning of some words. Write an **a** at the beginning of each word to make words that start with the short **a** sound.

apple   animal
ambulance   ant
alligator

SKILL: Recognizing the short sound of the vowel /a/.

page 51

Short Vowel Ee
E is a vowel. Vowels have two sounds, short and long. The short vowel **e** sounds like the **e** you hear in the middle of the word **bed**, and at the beginning of the word **egg**. Circle the pictures that have the short **e** sound in them.

page 52

Fill in the missing **e** to make words that start with the short **e** sound. Use the pictures to help you.

egg   bed
bell   elephant

SKILL: Recognizing the short vowel of the vowel /e/.

page 53

Short Vowel Ii
The letter **i** is a vowel. Vowels have two sounds, short and long. The short vowel **i** sounds like the **i** you hear in the middle of the word **pig**, and at the beginning of the word **igloo**. Circle the word with the short **i** sound that matches the picture. Next, write the word on the line under the picture.

wig big   lip pig   six hill
wig   pig   six

Write an **i** at the beginning of each word to make words that start with the short **i** sound.

igloo   iguana

SKILL: Recognizing the short sound of the vowel /i/.

page 54

Short Vowel Oo
The letter **o** is a vowel. Vowels have two sounds, short and long. The letter **o** sounds like the **o** you hear in the middle of the word **mop**, and at the beginning of the word **octopus**.
The octopus only wants to collect objects with the short **o** sound! Circle all the things that have the short **o** sound. Cross out the things that do not.

SKILL: Recognizing the short sound of the vowel /o/.

page 55

Short Vowel Uu
The letter **u** is a vowel. Vowels have two sounds, short and long. The short vowel **u** sounds like the **u** you hear in the middle of the word **sun**, and at the beginning of the word **up**. Fill in the missing letters to make words with the short **u** sound.

sun   bus
nut   cup / mug

SKILL: Recognizing the short sound of the vowel /u/.

page 56

Long Vowel Aa
The long vowel **a** sounds like the **a** you hear in the word **game**.
Connect the pictures with the long **a** sound by drawing a line from the first picture with the long **a** sound at the Start to the next, and then the next. See if you can make it to the Finish to win the game!

SKILL: Recognizing the long sound of the letter **a**.

page 57

Long Vowel Ee
The long vowel **e** sounds like the **e** you hear in the word **eagle**. The long **e** sound is sometimes written with **ee** or **ea**.
Draw a line from the picture to the word that matches it.

leaf
bee
seal
cheese

page 58

Long Vowel Ii
The long vowel **i** sounds like the **i** in the word **kite**. Fill in the missing **i** in the words on the kites. Draw strings from the kites to the matching pictures with the long **i** sound.

b_ike
t_ire
_ice cream
n_ine

page 59

Long Vowel Oo
The long vowel **o** sounds like the **o** in the word **boat**. Circle the things in the boat that have the long **o** sound. Cross out those that do not.

page 60

Long Vowel Uu
The long vowel **u** sounds like the **u** in the word **cube**. Make an X through the pictures with the long **u** sound. Did you get a tic-tac-toe?

Fill in the missing **u** to make a word that has the long **u** sound.

m_usic

page 61

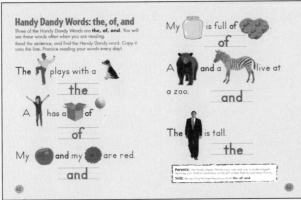

Handy Dandy Words: the, of, and
Three of the Handy Dandy Words are **the**, **of**, **and**. You will see these words often when you are reading.
Read the sentence, and find the Handy Dandy word. Copy it onto the line. Practice reading your words every day!

The ___ plays with a ___
the
A ___ has a ___ of ___.
of
My ___ and my ___ are red.
and

My ___ is full of ___
of
A ___ and a ___ live at a zoo.
and
The ___ is tall.
the

page 62

page 63

Handy Dandy Words: a, to, in
Three more Handy Dandy Words are **a**, **to**, **in**. Learning these words will make reading easier.
Write the Handy Dandy word in the sentence where it belongs. You will use each word only once!

The girl makes **a** snowman.
The dog is **in** the tub.
The kids are going **to** school.

a to in

page 64

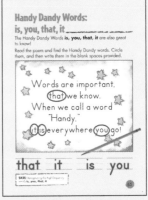

Handy Dandy Words: is, you, that, it
The Handy Dandy Words **is**, **you**, **that**, **it** are also great to know!
Read the poem and find the Handy Dandy words. Circle them, and then write them in the blank spaces provided.

Words are important,
(that) we know.
When we call a word
"Handy,"
(it) (is) everywhere (you) go!

that   it   is   you

page 65

Play ball!
The word **baseball** starts with the sound of the letter **b**. Fill in the missing **b** at the beginning of each word. Then circle all the words that start with the sound of the letter **b**.

boy
bat
ball

page 66

Pack the Car!
The word **car** starts with the letter **c**. In the word **car**, the **c** says the hard **c** sound.
Carrie can only pack the car with things that start with the letter **c** and have the hard **c** sound. Circle the things she should pack, and cross out those she shouldn't. Write the letter **c** in the space at the beginning of each word. Try to read the words!

cup
coat
can
candy

page 67

City Circus
The words **circus** and **city** start with the letter **c**. In these words the **c** says the soft sound of **c**.
Make your way from the city to the circus by following the path with the words that begin with the soft **c** sound. Write the letter **c** in the spaces to complete the words.

city
circus

page 68

Detective Dog
The word **dog** starts with the sound of the letter **d**. Fill in the missing **d** to complete each word.

d_uck
d_oor
d_oll
d_ice

page 69

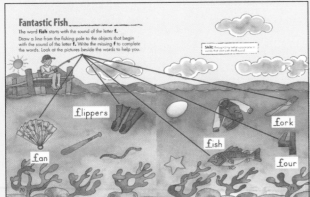

Fantastic Fish
The word **fish** starts with the sound of the letter **f**.
Draw a line from the fishing pole to the objects that begin with the sound of the letter **f**. Write the missing **f** to complete the words. Look at the pictures beside the words to help you.

flippers
fan
fish
fork
four

page 70

page 71

Go for the Gold
The word **gold** starts with the letter **g**. In the word **gold**, the **g** says the hard **g** sound.
Grace can only kick the soccer balls with pictures that start with the hard **g** sound. Color the soccer balls with pictures that start with the hard **g** sound. Write the missing **g** in each space.

grapes
gold

page 72

Soft Gg Sound
The word **giant** starts with the letter **g**. In the word **giant**, the **g** says the soft **g** sound.
Name of each picture and listen for the soft **g** sound. Write the letter **g** in each of the spaces below to complete the words.

giraffe   gem
giant   gym
gerbil

page 73

Helping Hands

The word **hand** starts with the sound of the letter **h.** Circle each picture that begins with the **h** sound, and cross out each picture that does not.

page 74

Juggling Jj's

The word **jar** starts with the sound of the letter **j.** Circle the pictures that start with the sound of the letter **j.** At the bottom, practice writing the **j** to make **j** words.

jump rope

jellybeans

page 75

Doors Galore!

The word **key** starts with the sound of the letter **k.** Kevin's key can only unlock the doors with things that begin with the sound of the letter **k.** Draw a line from Kevin's key to the doors with the correct pictures, then write the beginning letter **k** to make **k** words.

kettle

kangaroo

king

page 76

Lots of Locks!

The word **lock** starts with the sound of the letter **L.** Draw a line from the pictures that start with the sound of **l** to the lock in the center of the page. Practice writing **l**'s to finish the words that start with **l.** Use the pictures to help you read the words.

lion
lips
leg

page 77

Marvelous Mittens

The word **mitten** starts with the sound of the letter **m.** Help the mittens find their matches! Follow each mitten's string to lead it to its partner. Practice writing the letter **m** on the mittens, and fill in the missing **m** at the bottom of the page to make words that begin with the **m** sound.

mitten   match

page 78

Read All About It!

The word **newspaper** starts with the sound of the letter **n.** Look at the pictures in the newspaper, and color the pictures that begin with the sound of the letter **n.** Then fill in the missing **n** to complete the words. Look at the pictures for help.

nest

nickel

page 79

Prized Pigs!

The word **pig** starts with the sound of the letter **p.** Fill in the missing **p** to complete the word.

pig

The black and white pig won the contest. Help him circle a prize that begins with the **p** sound.

The pink pig came in second. She wants the prize that begins with the **p** sound. Circle the prize that she should choose.

The white pig got third place. He won a prize that begins with the **p** sound. Circle the prize that he won.

page 80

Words that Start with Qq

The word **quilt** starts with the sound of the letter **q.** The letter **q** is almost always paired with **u.** Fill in the missing **qu** to complete words that have the sound of the letter **q.** Then circle the pictures that match the words.

queen   quarter   quilt

page 81

Words that Start with Rr

The word **rabbit** starts with the sound of the letter **r.** Write the missing **r** to make words that begin with the sound of the letter **r.** Read the words, then draw lines from the words to the pictures that match them.

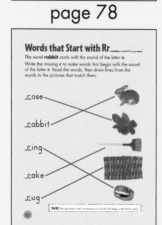

rose

rabbit

ring

rake

rug

page 82

Hungry Snake!

The word **snake** starts with the sound of the letter **s.** The snake has swallowed some objects. Color in the pictures that begin with the sound of the letter **s.** Fill in the missing **s** to complete the word.

snake

page 83

Terrific Turtles!

The word **turtle** starts with the sound of the letter **t.** Help the turtles choose the picture that begins with the sound of **t** in each row by circling it. At the bottom of each column, write the name of the picture you circled. Use the word bank at the bottom to help you write the words.

tent   ten   tie   tire

tire tent ten tie

page 84

Words that Start with Vv

The word **van** starts with the sound of the letter **v.** The van can only carry objects that start with the letter **v.** Write the letter **v** to complete the word. Then, load the van with the correct item! Draw lines to the van from the pictures that begin with the letter **v.**

van

page 85

Wagons and Wheelbarrows!

The words **wagon** and **wheelbarrow** start with the letter **w.** Circle the word that matches the picture in the wagon or wheelbarrow. Then write the word you circled on the line below.

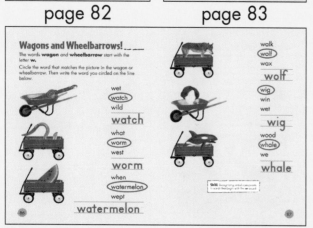

wet
watch
wild

watch

what
worm
west

worm

when
watermelon
wept

watermelon

walk
wolf
wax

wolf

wig
win
wet

wig

wood
whale
we

whale

page 86

page 87

Words that Start with Yy

The word **yak** starts with the sound of the letter **y.** Say the name of each picture, and read the words below it. Circle the word that matches the picture, and write the word on the lines.

yuck   yarn

yarn

yard   yak

yak

yes   yellow

yellow

yo-yo   you

yo-yo

page 88

Words that Start with Zz

The word **zebra** starts with the sound of the letter **z.** Write the correct word that starts with the sound of the letter **z** below each picture. Use the word bank to help you write the words. Cross out the words as you use them.

zebra   zigzag

zero   zipper

zebra zero zipper zigzag

page 89

Rhyme Time

page 90

Find a Rhyme

page 91

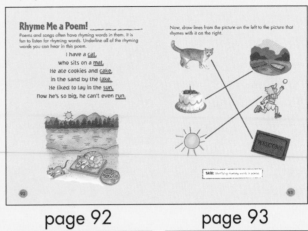
Rhyme Me a Poem!

page 92

page 93

Word Families

page 94

Word Family Farm

page 95

Writing Word Families

page 96

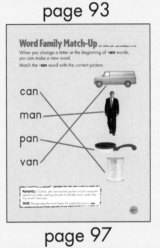
Word Family Match-Up

page 97

Word Family Recess!

page 98

Word Switch

page 99

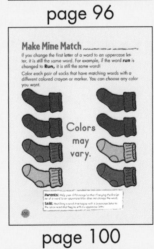
Make Mine Match

page 100

Tub Time

page 101

Birds of a Feather

page 102

Moving Day

page 103

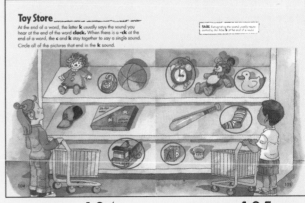
Toy Store

page 104

page 105

page 106
Here Comes the Mail
At the end of a word, the letter **l** or letters **ll** usually say the sound you hear at the end of the word **mail** or **ball**.
Add **-l** or **-ll** to the end of each word to complete them.

pail
sail
nail
ball
doll

page 107
Ending M's
At the end of a word, the letter **m** usually says the sound you hear at the end of the word **gum**.
Color all the shapes that have words ending with the **m** sound yellow. Color all the shapes that do not have words ending with the **m** sound red. Color the blank shapes blue.

page 108
Fun in the Sun!
At the end of a word, the letter **n** usually says the sound you hear at the end of the word **sun**.
Circle all of the words that end with the **n** sound. Then, practice writing the words that you found in the picture.

sun   ten   man
words will vary

page 109
In the Diner
At the end of a word, the letter **p** usually says the sound you hear at the end of the word **cup**.
Draw a line from the letter **p** that the server is carrying to the words that end in the **p** sound. At the bottom, fill in the missing p to form two words that end in the **p** sound. Use the pictures to help you.

map   cup

page 110
Give Me An "R"?
At the end of a word, the letter **r** usually says the sound you hear at the end of the word **cheer**.
Add the missing **r** to make words that end with the sound of **r**. Draw a line from each cheerleader's sign to the correct picture.

star
tour
flower
pear

page 111
Best Dressed
At the end of a word, the letter **s** usually says the sound that you hear at the end of the word **dress**.
Tess needs a new dress! Help her choose by coloring in the dresses with pictures that end in the **s** sound. Write the words for the pictures that end in **s** at the bottom.

grass   bus   kiss

page 112
Follow The Trail
At the end of a word, the letter **t** usually says the sound you hear at the end of the word **cat** and **rat**.
The cat is trying to find the rat. Draw a line through the pictures that end with the sound of **t** to lead the cat to it!

page 113
Fox in Box
The letter **x** at the end of the word usually says the sound almost like a **k** and **s** sound put together. You can hear it at the end of words like **fox** and **box**.
Which words end with the sound of **x**? Circle all of the pictures ending with the sound of **x** that you find in the boxes.

page 114
Change A Word
You can sometimes change the last letter of a word to make a new word.
Choose a different ending letter to make a new word that matches the picture. Write the new word on the lines.

hut (g,m)   hug
hot (p,g)   hop
pad (l,n)   pan
mat (n,d)   man

page 115
Building Words
When you change the last letter of a word, it changes the way you pronounce the word out loud. Cross out the final letter and add the new letter beside it to make a new word. Now write the word you just made. Circle the picture that shows the new word.

ra❌(m)   ram
ma❌(n)   man
ca❌(p)   cap
cu❌(b)   cub

page 116
What's the Word?
As you already know, you can sometimes change the first letter of a word to make a new word. Look at the words below and follow the directions. Write the new word in the space beside each sentence.

Write the word you make when you change the **d** in **day** to **p**.   pay

Write the word you make when you change the **s** in **set** to **j**.   jet

Write the word you make when you change the **z** in **zip** to **l**.   lip

page 117
Write the word you make when you change the **h** in **hog** to **d**.   dog

Write the word you make when you change the **h** in **hut** to **n**.   nut

Write the word you make when you change the **m** in **man** to **c**.   can

page 118
Vowel Prowl
You can also make new words by changing the vowel sound in the middle of a word.
Change the middle vowels in these words to make new words that match the picture. You will use the vowels **a, e, i, o, u**. You will use each vowel only one time.

bad   bed
bell   ball
pen   pin
big   bug
pet   pot

page 119
What's the Ending?
You can sometimes make new words by changing the last letter of a word.
Look at the word on the left. Change the ending letter of each word to the new letter in parentheses. Draw a line from each new word to its picture, then write the new word on the lines.

had(t)   rug
pet(n)   hat
run(g)   bat
bad(t)   pen